3230308491

ENDANGERED
SPECIES

CITY OF GLASGOW COLLEGE
North Hanover Street Library
60 North Hanover Street
Glasgow G1 2BP

0141 566 4132

ROCKPORT

©2011 by ricorico

All rights reserved. No part of this book may be reproduced in any form without written permission of the copyright owners. All images in this book have been reproduced with the knowledge and prior content of the artists concerned and no responsibility is accepted by producer, publisher, or printer for any infringement of copyright or otherwise, arising from the contents of this publication. Every effort has been made to ensure that credits accurately comply with information supplied.

First published in 2011 in the USA by
Rockport Publishers, a member of
Quayside Publishing Group
100 Cummings Center / 406-L
Beverly, Massachusetts 01915
USA
Phone: 987-282-9590
Fax: 978-283-2742
www.rockpub.com

Illustrations for Templates: Curl, Miwa Hirose, Yuki Kobayashi
Illustrations for Components: RYOKEN
Illustrations for Examples In Use: Andrew Pothecary (forbiddencolour)
Art Direction: Katsuya Moriizumi
Design: Andrew Pothecary (forbiddencolour)
Translation: Alma Reyes (ricorico)
Editing: Rico Komanoya (ricorico)

ISBN-13: 978-1-59253-665-8
ISBN-10: 1-59253-665-4

10 9 8 7 6 5 4 3 2 1

Printed in China

ENDANGERED SPECIES

by **ricorico**

CONTENTS

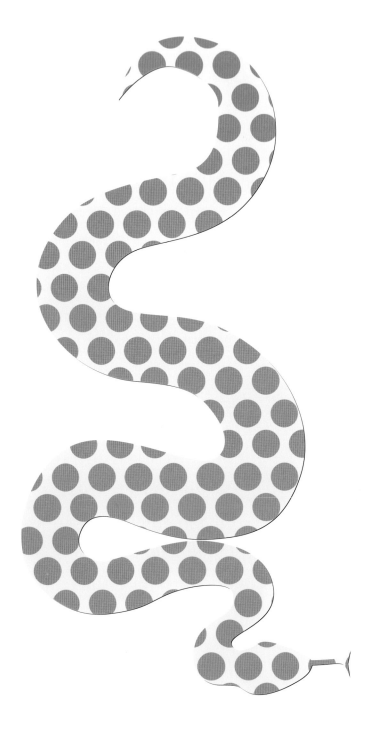

HOW TO USE THIS BOOK
AND THE CD-ROM

This volume is a collection of usable artworks for designers and artists that features hundreds of popular and thematic subjects. It is designed to highlight the following categories:

Templates: *These are designed to be used as is, or to be manipulated, edited, and/or modified as preferred, for your personal and professional use. This chapter lies in the middle section of the book, and shows one item per page in order for you to see its details.*

Examples of Applied Templates: *In the following page, and before the Templates chapter begins, there are seventeen variations of examples of the applied templates illustrated in this chapter. From printed materials to interior decoration items, you can see how effectively the entire template drawing or a part of it can be rendered.*

Components: *All templates are made of multiple components introduced in this chapter. These components can be used as single or combined items, or joined with other components from other templates, to create your own unique and original artworks. The file numbers of the components correspond to the page number of the template illustrations.*

CD-ROM: *All the original files for the templates and components are digitally archived both in JPEG and in Adobe Illustrator vector files in the CD-ROM that is attached at the end of the book.*

EXAMPLES

Coffee cup

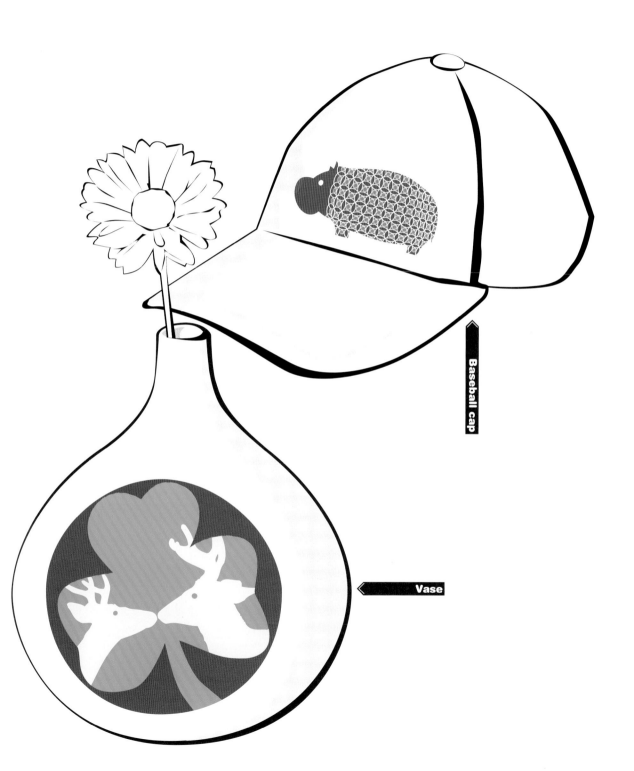

Baseball cap

Vase

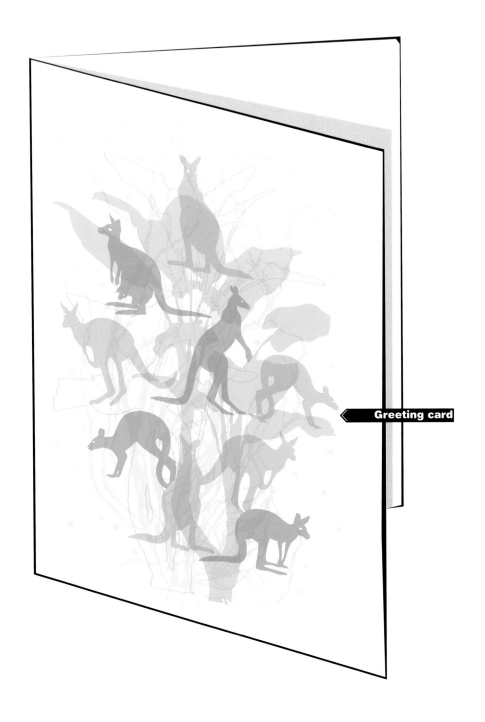

Greeting card

Bookmark

Calendar

Lampshade

Dust jacket

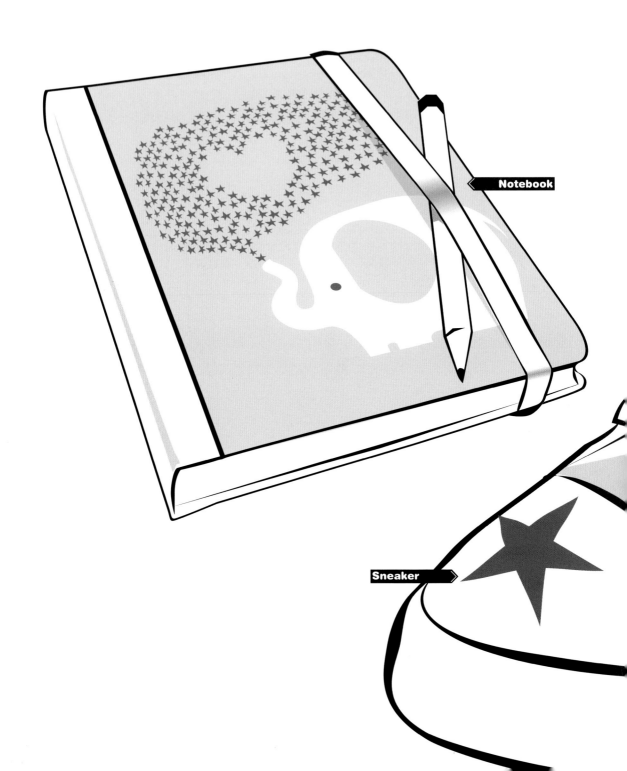

Notebook

Sneaker

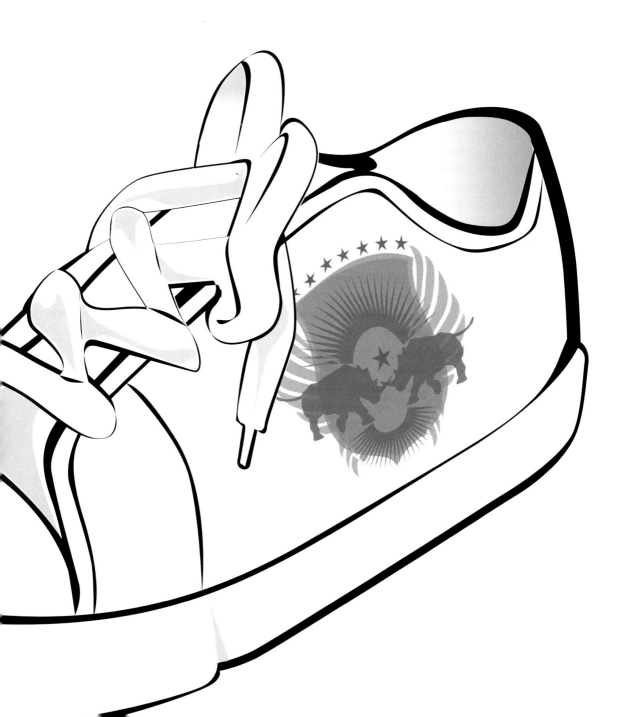

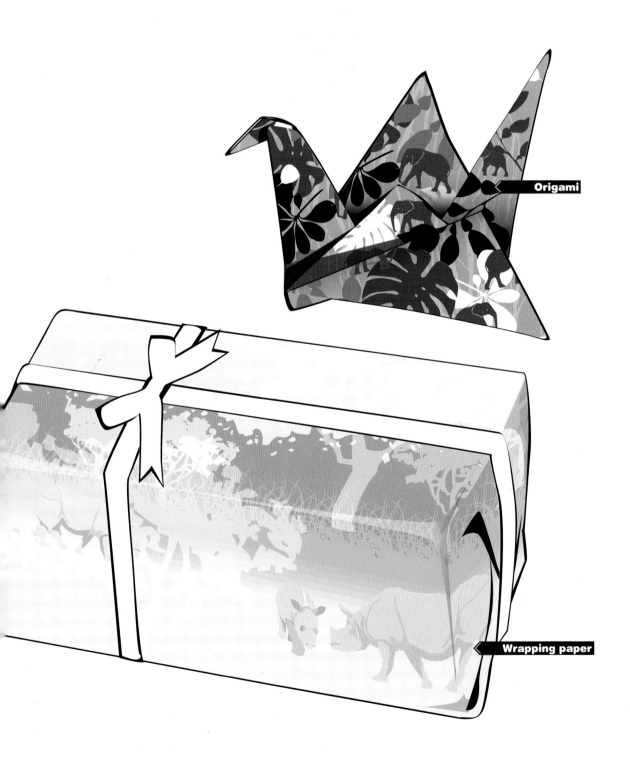

Origami

Wrapping paper

CITY OF GLASGOW COLLEGE
North Hanover Street Library
60 North Hanover Street
Glasgow G1 2BP
0141 566 4132

Umbrella

Tote bag

Photo frame

TEMPLATES

TEMPLATES

TEMPLATES

TEMPLATES

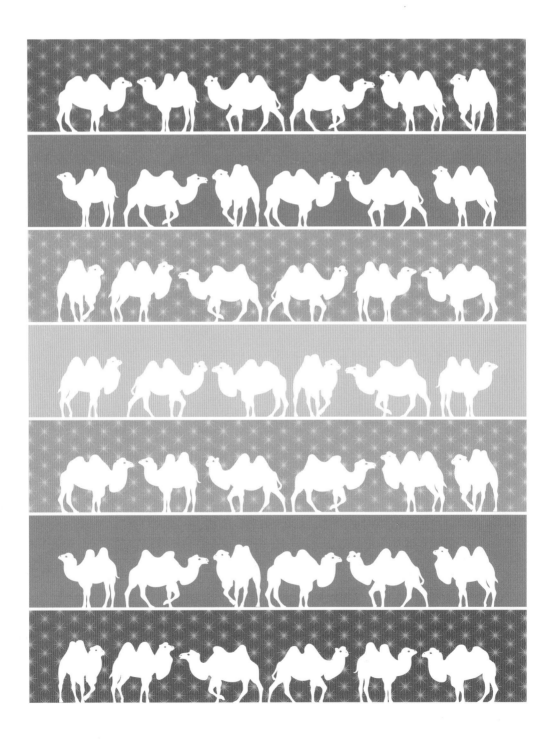

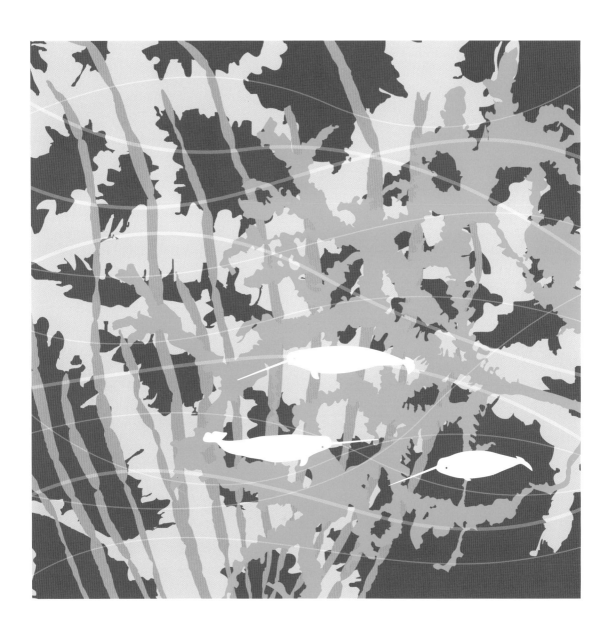

TEMPLATES

ES_T36

TEMPLATES

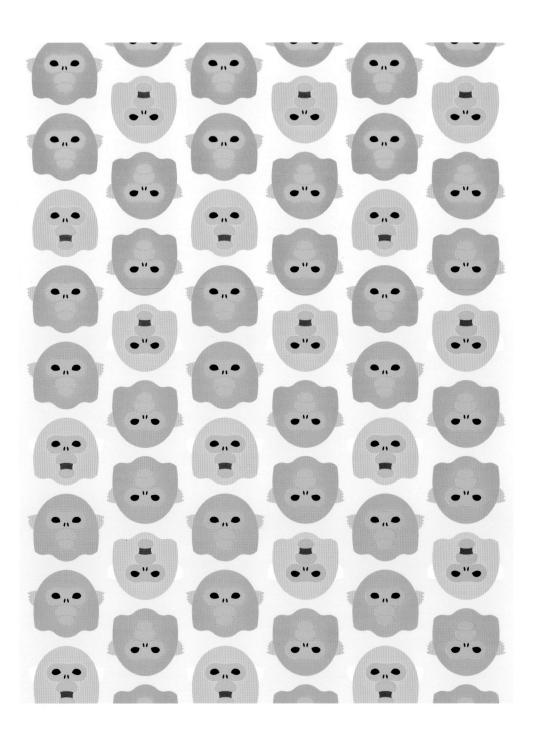

BISON

ES_T40

ES_T42

TEMPLATES

ES_T48

TEMPLATES

TEMPLATES

TEMPLATES

TEMPLATES

ES_T58

TEMPLATES

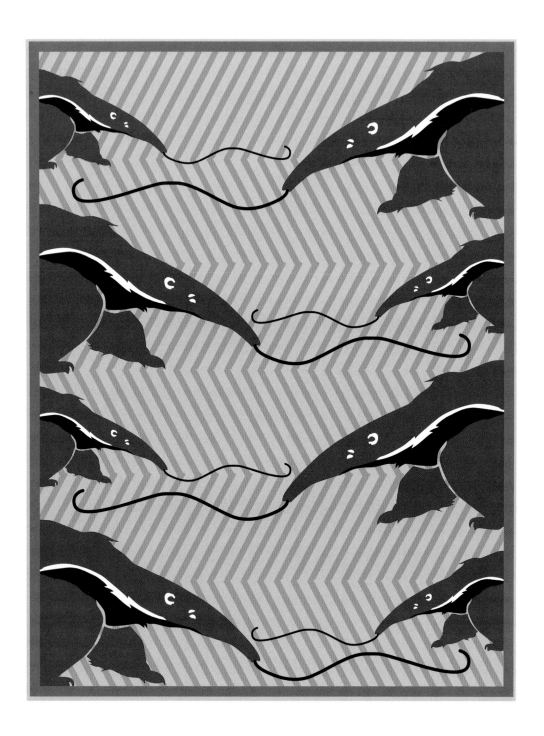

TEMPLATES

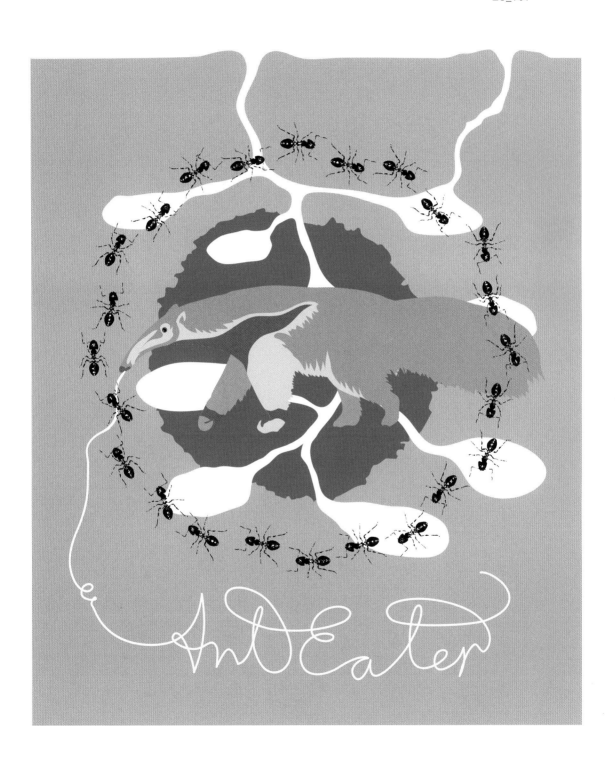

ES_T62

TEMPLATES

ES_T64

TEMPLATES

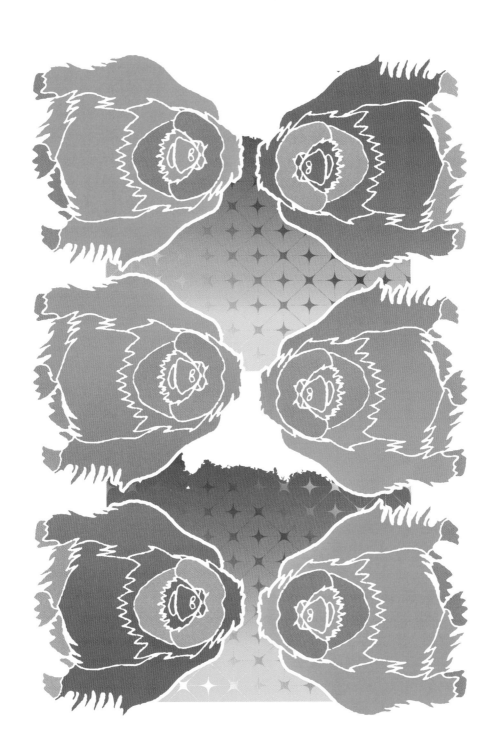

ES_T66

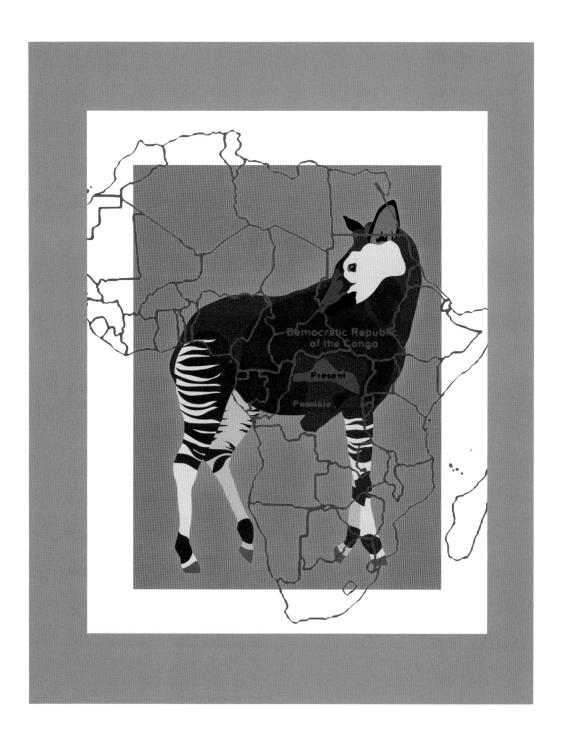

TEMPLATES

TEMPLATES

TEMPLATES

ES_T74   # TEMPLATES

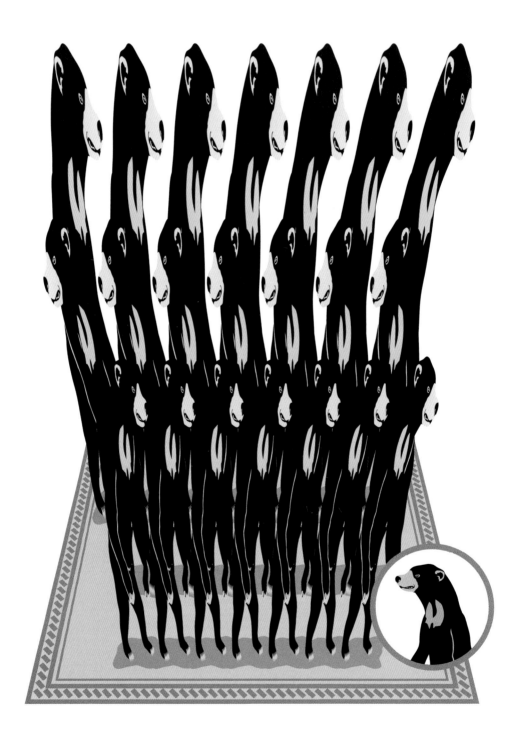

ES_T78

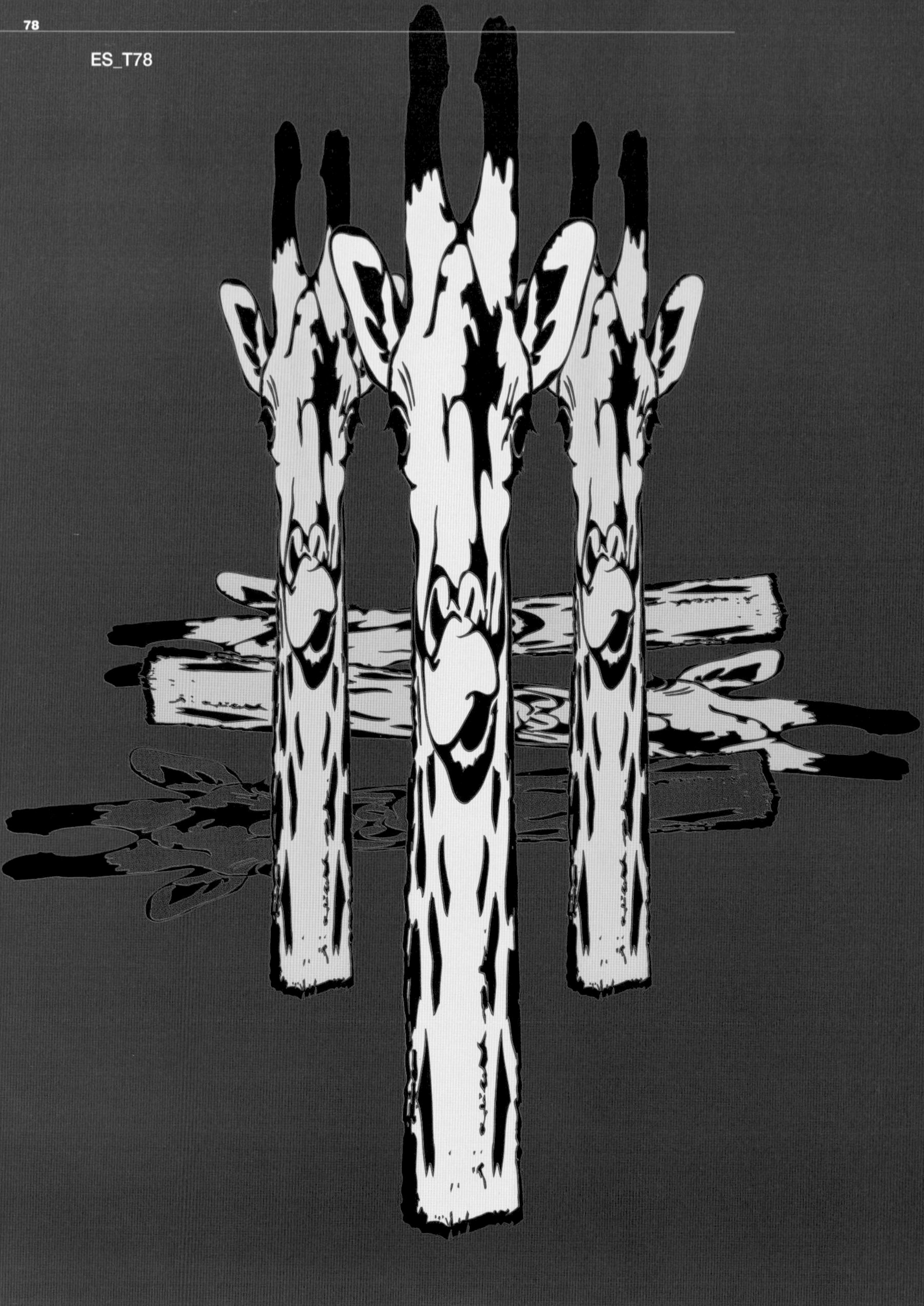

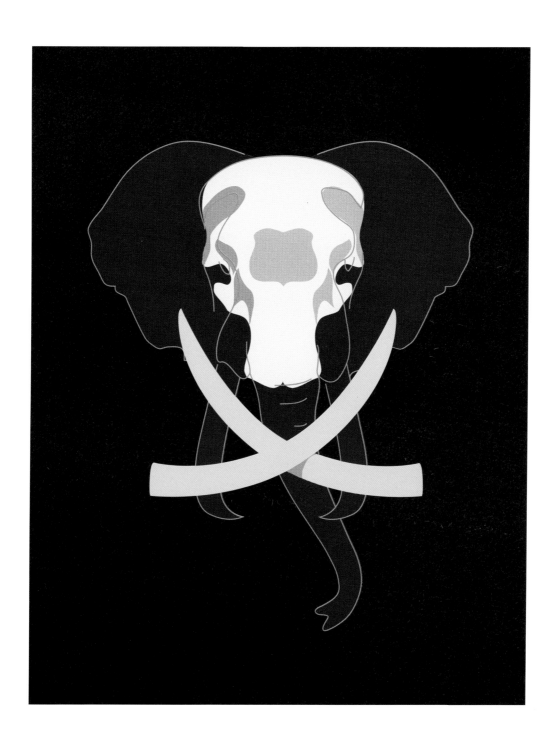

ES_T80

TEMPLATES

TEMPLATES

TEMPLATES

TEMPLATES

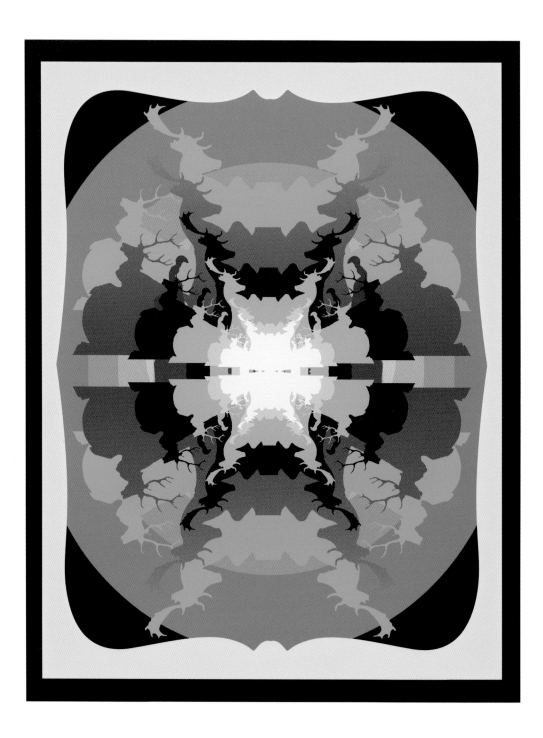

ES_T90

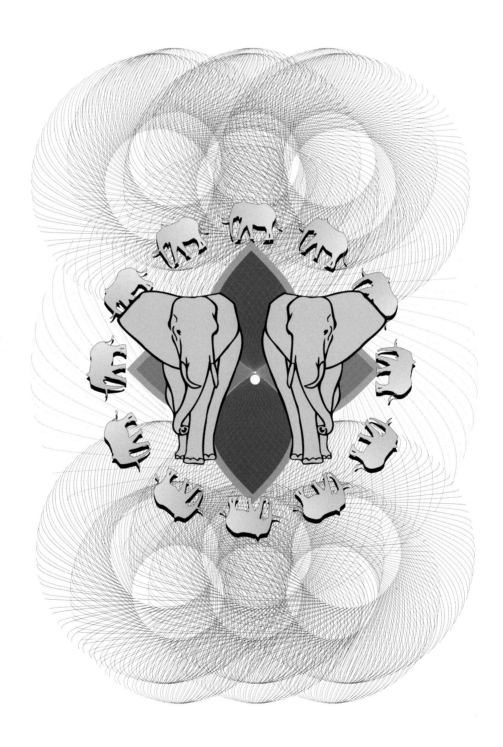

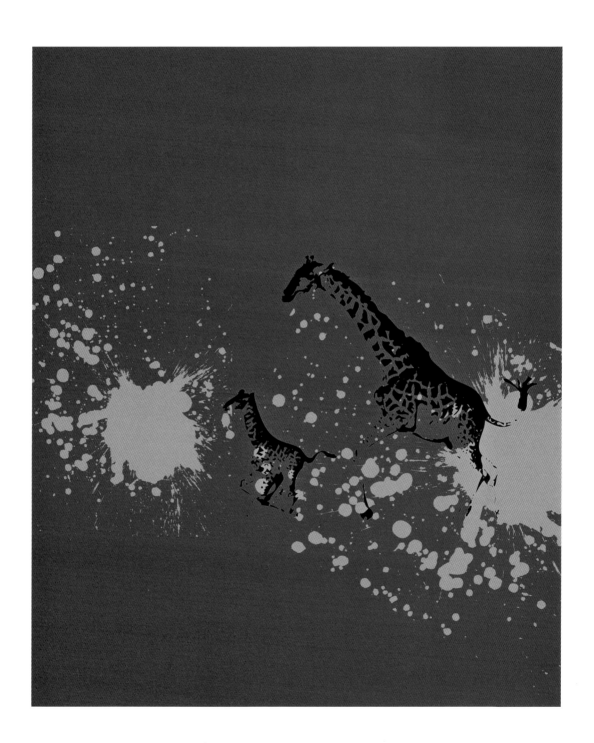

TEMPLATES

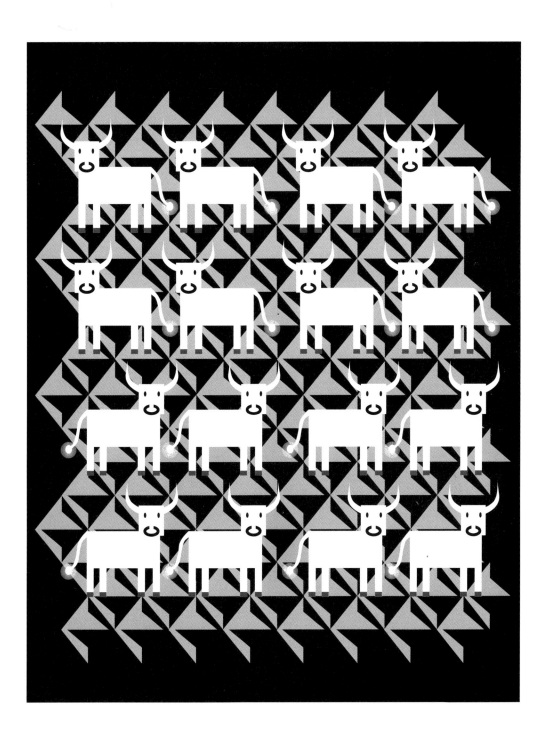

TEMPLATES

TEMPLATES

TEMPLATES

ES_T103

TEMPLATES

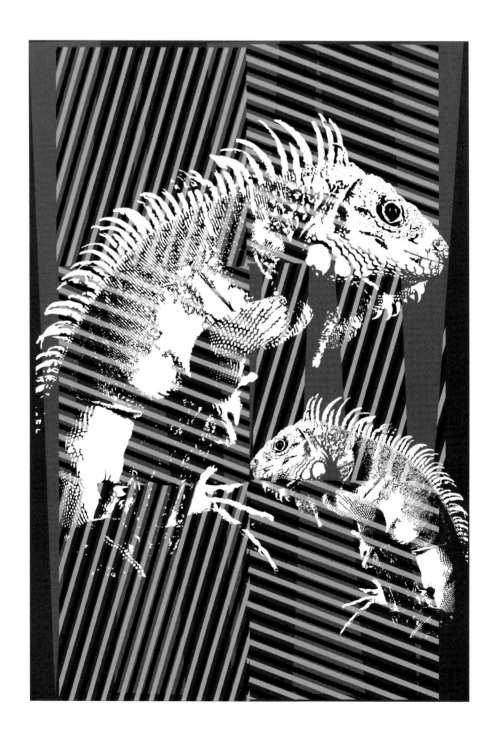

ES_T106

TEMPLATES

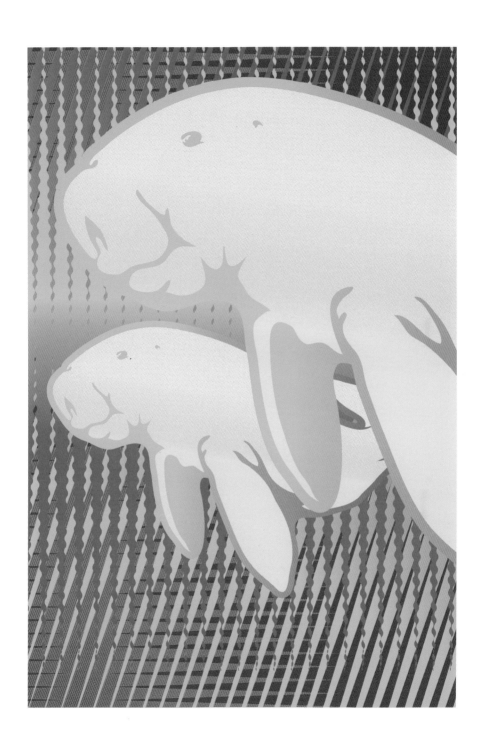

TEMPLATES

ES_T110

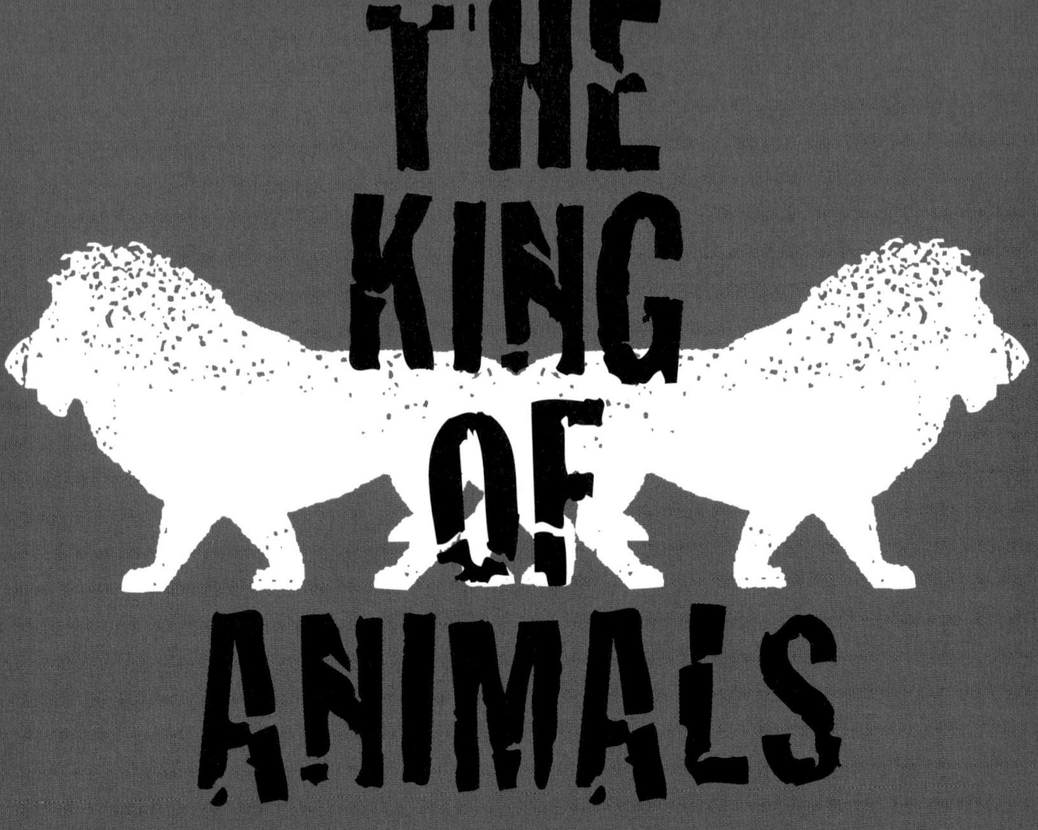

ES_T112

TEMPLATES

TEMPLATES

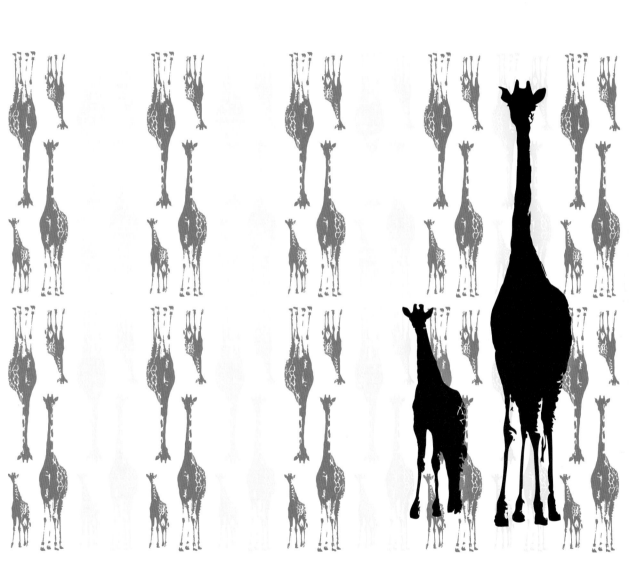

ES_T116

TEMPLATES

TEMPLATES

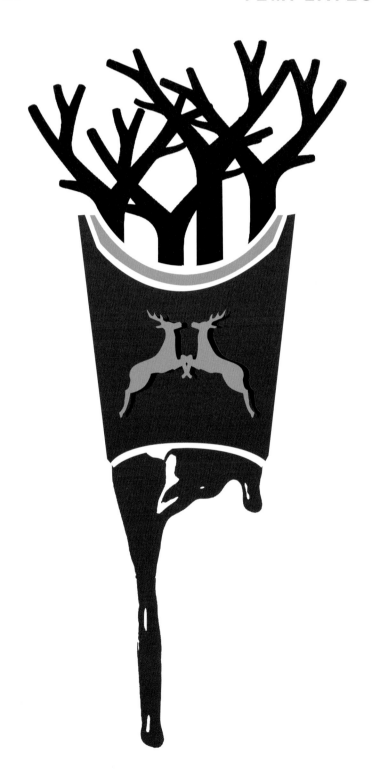

COMPONENTS

COMPONENTS

File name: ES_T26_01
Page 26

File name: ES_T26_02
Page 26

File name: ES_T26_03
Page 26

File name: ES_T26_04
Page 26

File name: ES_T27_01
Page 27

File name: ES_T27_02
Page 27

File name: ES_T27_03
Page 27

File name: ES_T27_04
Page 27

File name: ES_T27_05
Page 27

File name: ES_T27_06
Page 27

File name: ES_T27_07
Page 27

File name: ES_T27_08
Page 27

File name: ES_T28_01
Page 28

File name: ES_T28_02
Page 28

File name: ES_T28_03
Page 28

File name: ES_T28_04
Page 28

File name: ES_T28_05
Page 28

File name: ES_T28_06
Page 28

File name: ES_T28_07
Page 28

File name: ES_T29_01
Page 29

File name: ES_T29_02
Page 29

File name: ES_T29_03
Page 29

File name: ES_T29_04
Page 29

File name: ES_T29_05
Page 29

COMPONENTS

File name: ES_T29_06
Page 29

File name: ES_T29_07
Page 29

File name: ES_T30_01
Page 30

File name: ES_T30_02
Page 30

File name: ES_T30_03
Page 30

File name: ES_T31_01
Page 31

File name: ES_T31_02
Page 31

File name: ES_T31_03
Page 31

File name: ES_T31_04
Page 31

File name: ES_T31_05
Page 31

File name: ES_T31_06
Page 31

File name: ES_T31_07
Page 31

File name: ES_T32_01
Page 32

File name: ES_T32_02
Page 32

File name: ES_T32_03
Page 32

File name: ES_T32_04
Page 32

File name: ES_T32_05
Page 32

File name: ES_T32_06
Page 32

File name: ES_T33_01
Page 33

File name: ES_T33_02
Page 33

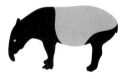

File name: ES_T33_03
Page 33

File name: ES_T33_04
Page 33

File name: ES_T33_05
Page 33

File name: ES_T36_01
Page 36

COMPONENTS

File name: ES_T36_02
Page 36

File name: ES_T37_01
Page 37

File name: ES_T37_02
Page 37

File name: ES_T37_03
Page 37

File name: ES_T37_04
Page 37

File name: ES_T38_01
Page 38

File name: ES_T39_01
Page 39

File name: ES_T39_02
Page 39

File name: ES_T40_01
Page 40

File name: ES_T40_02
Page 40

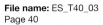

File name: ES_T40_03
Page 40

File name: ES_T41_01
Page 41

File name: ES_T41_02
Page 41

File name: ES_T41_03
Page 41

File name: ES_T42_01
Page 42

File name: ES_T43_01
Page 43

File name: ES_T43_02
Page 43

File name: ES_T43_03
Page 43

File name: ES_T46_01
Page 46

File name: ES_T46_02
Page 46

File name: ES_T47_01
Page 47

File name: ES_T47_02
Page 47

File name: ES_T48_01
Page 48

File name: ES_T48_02
Page 48

COMPONENTS

File name: ES_T48_03
Page 48

File name: ES_T49_01
Page 49

File name: ES_T50_01
Page 50

File name: ES_T50_02
Page 50

File name: ES_T51_01
Page 51

File name: ES_T51_02
Page 51

File name: ES_T52_01
Page 52

File name: ES_T52_02
Page 52

File name: ES_T53_01
Page 53

File name: ES_T53_02
Page 53

File name: ES_T53_03
Page 53

File name: ES_T53_04
Page 53

File name: ES_T53_05
Page 53

File name: ES_T53_06
Page 53

File name: ES_T53_07
Page 53

File name: ES_T53_08
Page 53

JAGUAR

File name: ES_T53_09
Page 53

File name: ES_T54_01
Page 54

File name: ES_T54_01
Page 54

File name: ES_T56_01
Page 56

File name: ES_T56_02
Page 56

File name: ES_T56_03
Page 56

File name: ES_T56_04
Page 56

File name: ES_T56_05
Page 56

COMPONENTS

File name: ES_T57_01
Page 57

Squirrel

File name: ES_T57_02
Page 57

File name: ES_T58_01
Page 58

File name: ES_T59_01
Page 59

File name: ES_T60_01
Page 60

File name: ES_T61_01
Page 61

File name: ES_T61_02
Page 61

File name: ES_T61_03
Page 61

File name: ES_T61_04
Page 61

File name: ES_T62_01
Page 62

File name: ES_T62_02
Page 62

File name: ES_T63_01
Page 63

File name: ES_T63_02
Page 63

File name: ES_T63_03
Page 63

File name: ES_T63_04
Page 63

File name: ES_T64_01
Page 64

File name: ES_T64_02
Page 64

File name: ES_T64_03
Page 64

File name: ES_T64_04
Page 64

File name: ES_T65_01
Page 65

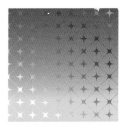

File name: ES_T65_02
Page 65

File name: ES_T66_01
Page 66

File name: ES_T67_01
Page 67

File name: ES_T67_02
Page 67

COMPONENTS

File name: ES_T68_01
Page 68

File name: ES_T69_01
Page 69

File name: ES_T70_01
Page 70

File name: ES_T70_02
Page 70

File name: ES_T71_01
Page 71

File name: ES_T71_02
Page 71

File name: ES_T71_03
Page 71

File name: ES_T72_01
Page 72

File name: ES_T72_02
Page 72

File name: ES_T72_03
Page 72

File name: ES_T72_04
Page 72

File name: ES_T72_05
Page 72

File name: ES_T72_06
Page 72

File name: ES_T72_07
Page 72

File name: ES_T73_01
Page 73

File name: ES_T73_02
Page 73

File name: ES_T73_03
Page 73

File name: ES_T73_04
Page 73

File name: ES_T73_05
Page 73

File name: ES_T74_01
Page 74

File name: ES_T74_02
Page 74

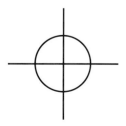

File name: ES_T74_03
Page 74

File name: ES_T74_04
Page 74

File name: ES_T75_01
Page 75

COMPONENTS

File name: ES_T76_01
Page 76

File name: ES_T77_01
Page 77

File name: ES_T78_01
Page 78

File name: ES_T79_01
Page 79

File name: ES_T79_02
Page 79

File name: ES_T80_01
Page 80

File name: ES_T80_02
Page 80

File name: ES_T80_03
Page 80

File name: ES_T80_04
Page 80

File name: ES_T80_05
Page 80

File name: ES_T80_06
Page 80

File name: ES_T81_01
Page 81

File name: ES_T81_02
Page 81

File name: ES_T81_03
Page 81

File name: ES_T82_01
Page 82

File name: ES_T82_02
Page 82

File name: ES_T82_03
Page 82

File name: ES_T82_04
Page 82

File name: ES_T83_01
Page 83

File name: ES_T83_02
Page 83

File name: ES_T83_03
Page 83

File name: ES_T83_04
Page 83

File name: ES_T83_05
Page 83

File name: ES_T83_06
Page 83

COMPONENTS

File name: ES_T86_01
Page 86

File name: ES_T86_02
Page 86

File name: ES_T86_03
Page 86

File name: ES_T86_04
Page 86

File name: ES_T86_05
Page 86

File name: ES_T86_06
Page 86

File name: ES_T86_07
Page 86

File name: ES_T86_08
Page 86

File name: ES_T87_01
Page 87

File name: ES_T87_02
Page 87

File name: ES_T87_03
Page 87

File name: ES_T87_04
Page 87

File name: ES_T87_05
Page 87

File name: ES_T87_06
Page 87

File name: ES_T88_01
Page 88

File name: ES_T88_01
Page 88

File name: ES_T89_01
Page 89

File name: ES_T90_01
Page 90

File name: ES_T90_02
Page 90

File name: ES_T90_03
Page 90

File name: ES_T90_04
Page 90

File name: ES_T91_01
Page 91

File name: ES_T91_02
Page 91

File name: ES_T91_01
Page 91

COMPONENTS

File name: ES_T92_01
Page 92

File name: ES_T92_02
Page 92

File name: ES_T93_01
Page 93

File name: ES_T94_01
Page 94

File name: ES_T94_02
Page 94

File name: ES_T94_03
Page 94

File name: ES_T95_01
Page 95

File name: ES_T95_02
Page 95

File name: ES_T95_03
Page 95

File name: ES_T95_04
Page 95

File name: ES_T95_05
Page 95

File name: ES_T95_06
Page 95

File name: ES_T95_07
Page 95

File name: ES_T96_01
Page 96

File name: ES_T96_02
Page 96

File name: ES_T97_01
Page 97

File name: ES_T100_01
Page 100

File name: ES_T101_01
Page 101

File name: ES_T102_01
Page 102

File name: ES_T103_01
Page 103

File name: ES_T104_01
Page 104

File name: ES_T105_01
Page 105

File name: ES_T106_01
Page 106

File name: ES_T106_02
Page 106

COMPONENTS

File name: ES_T107_01
Page 107

File name: ES_T108_01
Page 108

File name: ES_T109_01
Page 109

File name: ES_T109_02
Page 109

File name: ES_T109_03
Page 109

File name: ES_T110_01
Page 110

File name: ES_T110_02
Page 110

File name: ES_T111_01
Page 111

File name: ES_T111_02
Page 111

File name: ES_T112_01
Page 112

File name: ES_T113_01
Page 113

File name: ES_T113_02
Page 113

File name: ES_T113_03
Page 113

File name: ES_T114_01
Page 114

File name: ES_T114_02
Page 114

File name: ES_T115_01
Page 115

File name: ES_T116_01
Page 116

File name: ES_T116_02
Page 116

File name: ES_T116_03
Page 116

File name: ES_T117_01
Page 117

File name: ES_T117_02
Page 117

File name: ES_T118_01
Page 118

File name: ES_T118_02
Page 118

File name: ES_T118_03
Page 118

License Agreement for the CD-ROM Files

Licenser: ricorico

1. License
Licenser hereby grants a non-exclusive and non-transferable right and license to use the Templates and Components files in the CD-ROM (hereinafter referred to as "Files") to a customer who purchased the book Bones and Skulls (hereinafter referred to as "Book"), and who agreed to the terms and conditions of this Agreement (hereinafter referred to as "User").

The User may process, modify, and/or edit the Files included in the CD-ROM or distribute them as a single file or in combination with other materials on a printed matter as design material in the User's work, such as:
  a. digital media, including websites.
  b. graphics for shop interiors and signs.
  c. leaflets, flyers, posters, direct mail, catalogues, pamphlets, and other tools for advertisement or sales promotion.
  d. goods, clothes, greeting cards, business cards, and other articles for personal production and use. The files may be used for personal, professional, and commercial purposes, provided that the articles produced are not offered for sale. The User may not sell articles made with the Files even when of a personal nature. Please read the following Limitations carefully:

2. Limitations
The User is not licensed to do any of the following:
  a. License, or otherwise by any means permit, any other person to use the Files.
  b. Use the Files for commercial production of postcards, business cards, or any other articles, or sell any such articles made using the Files.
  c. Provide downloading services using the Files (including greeting card services).
  d. Use the Files in order to produce any software or any other objects for sale.
  e. Acquire the copyright in any material in the Files or any objects created using the Files.
  f. Use the Files to create obscene, scandalous, abusive or slanderous works.

3. Copyright and Other Intellectual Property
ricorico and its suppliers reserve the copyright and other intellectual property rights in the Files. When specifying the User of a product made using the Files, please also indicate "© 2010 ricorico".

4. Exclusion of Damages
In no event shall Rockport Publishers and ricorico be liable for any damages whatsoever (including but not limited to, damages for loss of profit or loss of the file contents) related to the use or inability to use the Files or use the materials in the Files.

5. Termination of this License Agreement
If the User breaches any of the articles in this Agreement, Rockport Publishers and ricorico have the right to withdraw the User's License granted on the basis hereof.

AB●UT THE AUTH●R

ricoricio *is a Tokyo-based book packaging company established in 2009. They have been actively producing books in the area of graphic design, photography, craft, pop culture, and manga, including two titles that they also authored.*